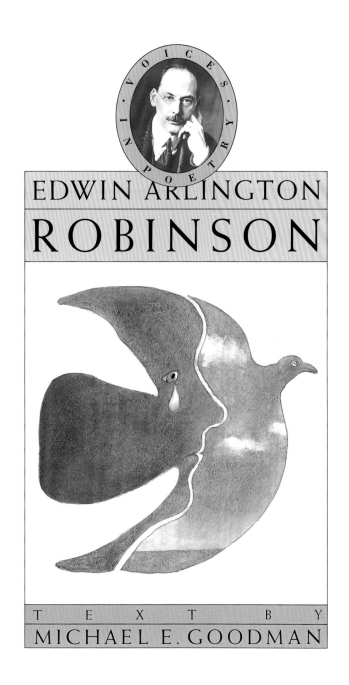

VOICES · IN · POETRY

EDWIN ARLINGTON
ROBINSON

TEXT BY
MICHAEL E. GOODMAN

ILLUSTRATIONS BY
ETIENNE DELESSERT

CREATIVE EDUCATION

DEAR FRIENDS

*D*ear friends, reproach me not for what I do,

Nor counsel me, nor pity me; nor say

That I am wearing half my life away

For bubble-work that only fools pursue.

And if my bubbles be too small for you,

Blow bigger then your own: the games we play

To fill the frittered minutes of a day,

Good glasses are to read the spirit through.

And whoso reads may get him some shrewd skill;

And some unprofitable scorn resign,

To praise the very thing that he deplores;

So, friends (dear friends), remember, if you will,

The shame I win for singing is all mine,

The gold I miss for dreaming is all yours.

From *The Children of the Night*

I N T R O D U C T I O N

"*I have presentiments. One of them is that the fellows who know me best are not going to forget me and another is that I am going to do something before I am through. . . . I shall never be a Prominent Citizen and I thank God for that, but I shall be something just as good perhaps and possibly a little more permanent.*"

Young poet Edwin Arlington Robinson wrote these words in a letter to a close friend in 1895, the year he sold his first poem for the grand sum of seven dollars.

Robinson's faith in his ability and his art seems prophetic today, but it took many years for him to earn a permanent place in American literature. He was nearly fifty years old before critics began to respect his talent, and nearly sixty before the public accepted him. Still, he stuck with his craft, overcoming personal tragedies and loneliness, living in near poverty much of his life, and refusing to be deterred when his poetry was either ignored or attacked.

During his lifetime, Robinson produced nearly one thousand pages of verse, more than almost any other American poet. He used old forms—sonnets, villanelles, octaves, and blank verse—in an entirely new way. In all of his work, Robinson used an original style and language to ponder the difficulties of human existence and the frailties of modern-day people. In so doing, he helped lay a foundation on which many other twentieth-century American poets could build.

CLIFF KLINGENHAGEN

*C*liff Klingenhagen had me in to dine

With him one day; and after soup and meat,

And all the other things there were to eat,

Cliff took two glasses and filled one with wine

And one with wormwood. Then, without a sign

For me to choose at all, he took the draught

Of bitterness himself, and lightly quaffed

It off, and said the other one was mine.

And when I asked him what the deuce he meant

By doing that, he only looked at me

And smiled, and said it was a way of his.

And though I know the fellow, I have spent

Long time a-wondering when I shall be

As happy as Cliff Klingenhagen is.

From *The Children of the Night*

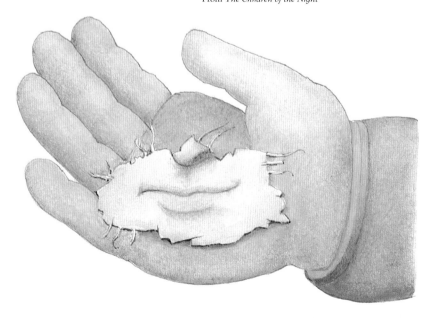

CHILDHOOD

$\mathcal{E}$dwin Arlington Robinson was born on December 22, 1869, in the tiny village of Head Tide, Maine. He was the third son of Edward and Mary Palmer Robinson. Both parents came from old New England stock, and Robinson's mother was a direct descendant of Anne Bradstreet, one of the earliest American poets.

The Robinsons took almost six months to choose a name for their new son. Finally, a visitor from Arlington, Massachusetts, suggested Edwin. Mary Robinson liked the choice so much that she honored the visitor by adding Arlington as the boy's middle name.

Before Edwin was a year old, his family moved to nearby Gardiner, Maine, a busy lumber and textile center with a population of 4,500. There his father became a prominent businessman. Edwin's two older brothers, Dean and Herman, received most of his father's attention, while the youngest son, shy and quiet, was sometimes almost forgotten. Edwin turned to reading mystery and adventure stories as a way to escape his loneliness.

Edward Robinson was a strong-willed man who made most of the decisions for the family. He decided that Dean would become a doctor and that Herman would take over the family's business interests. He wondered what to do with Edwin. The boy loved reading, but his mind often wandered in school or at home, and he didn't seem self-confident enough to become a businessman. Edward decided that going to college would be a waste for the boy. Instead, Edwin was required to take only practical courses in high school to prepare for the world of work. Edwin soon regretted going along with his father's wishes but did not have the courage to rebel.

The poet's birthplace, Head Tide, Maine.

"My father was to me a mighty stranger—

Fearsome, but always on the side of right

As he discerned it. There were some collisions

Between us, and a few sparks, though no fire

That ever burned enough to make a scar.

For the most part he let me go my way;

And when the way was hard, I made it so.

We'll say that many are better and some worse

Than I was then."

From the epic poem
Roman Bartholow

*A*s a teenager, Edwin was tall and lanky and too clumsy to be good at sports. Growing so fast, his bones often ached, and he seemed to tire faster than many of his friends. He liked playing word games and collecting bugs more than running, skating, or swimming. One of his favorite games was competing with friends to see who could find the longest word in the Bible or a school book. He won one contest with the word "Nebuchadnezzar."

Edwin had begun writing poems when he was eleven years old, but when his classmates made fun of his poetry, he tossed all of his early verses into the school furnace. He kept writing, though, and by the time he reached high school, a Gardiner physician and amateur poet named Alanson Tucker Schumann took note of him. Dr. Schumann had organized a local literary group, which he encouraged the young poet to join. The group became a haven of warmth and acceptance for the young man.

Under Dr. Schumann's influence, Edwin began experimenting with old French forms such as the villanelle and the ballade. These forms required a poet to follow intricate rhyme and rhythm patterns. Robinson enjoyed working within these complex restrictions and developed a technical excellence that was to characterize his work throughout his career.

Robinson's portrait in his high school yearbook, 1888.

BALLADE OF BROKEN FLUTES

(To A. T. Schumann)

In dreams I crossed a barren land,
    A land of ruin, far away;
Around me hung on every hand
    A deathful stillness of decay;
    And silent, as in bleak dismay
That song should thus forsaken be,
    On that forgotten ground there lay
The broken flutes of Arcady.

The forest that was all so grand
    When pipes and tabors had their sway
Stood leafless now, a ghostly band
    Of skeletons in cold array.
    A lonely surge of ancient spray
Told of an unforgetful sea,
    But iron blows had hushed for aye
The broken flutes of Arcady.

No more by summer breezes fanned,
    The place was desolate and gray;
But still my dream was to command
    New life into that shrunken clay.
    I tried it. And you scan to-day,
With uncommiserating glee,
    The songs of one who strove to play
The broken flutes of Arcady.

ENVOY

So, Rock, I join the common fray,
    To fight where Mammon may decree;
And leave, to crumble as they may,
    The broken flutes of Arcady.

From The Children of the Night

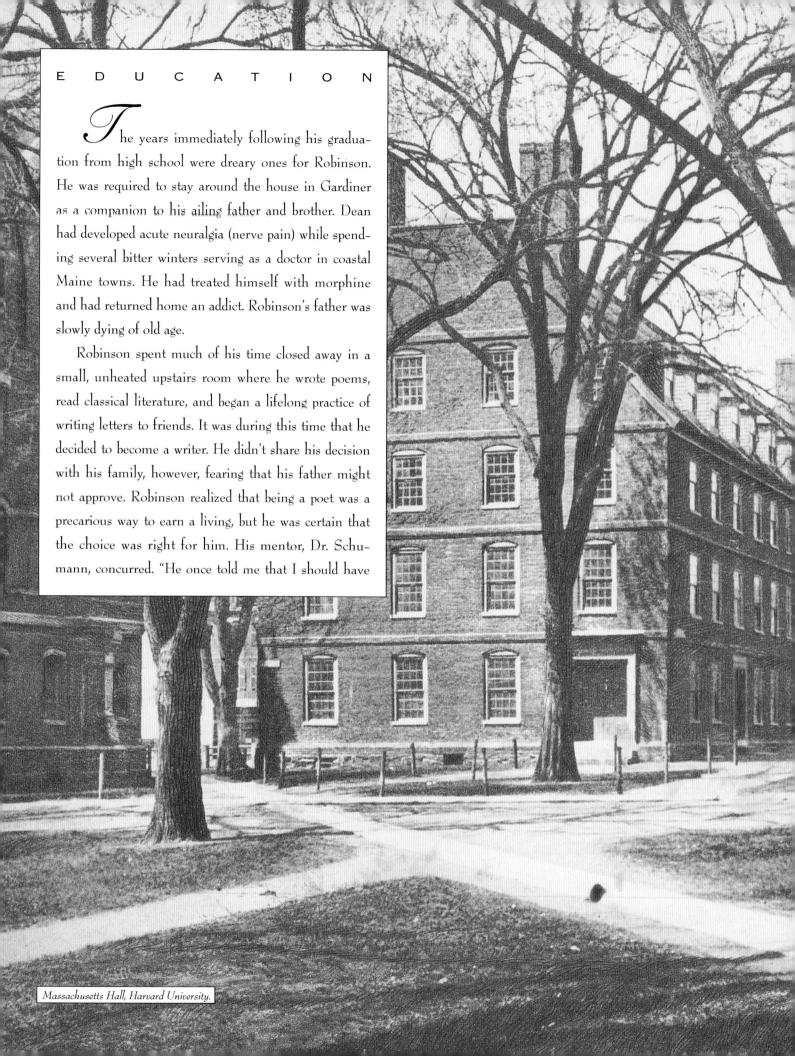

*T*he years immediately following his graduation from high school were dreary ones for Robinson. He was required to stay around the house in Gardiner as a companion to his ailing father and brother. Dean had developed acute neuralgia (nerve pain) while spending several bitter winters serving as a doctor in coastal Maine towns. He had treated himself with morphine and had returned home an addict. Robinson's father was slowly dying of old age.

Robinson spent much of his time closed away in a small, unheated upstairs room where he wrote poems, read classical literature, and began a lifelong practice of writing letters to friends. It was during this time that he decided to become a writer. He didn't share his decision with his family, however, fearing that his father might not approve. Robinson realized that being a poet was a precarious way to earn a living, but he was certain that the choice was right for him. His mentor, Dr. Schumann, concurred. "He once told me that I should have

Massachusetts Hall, Harvard University.

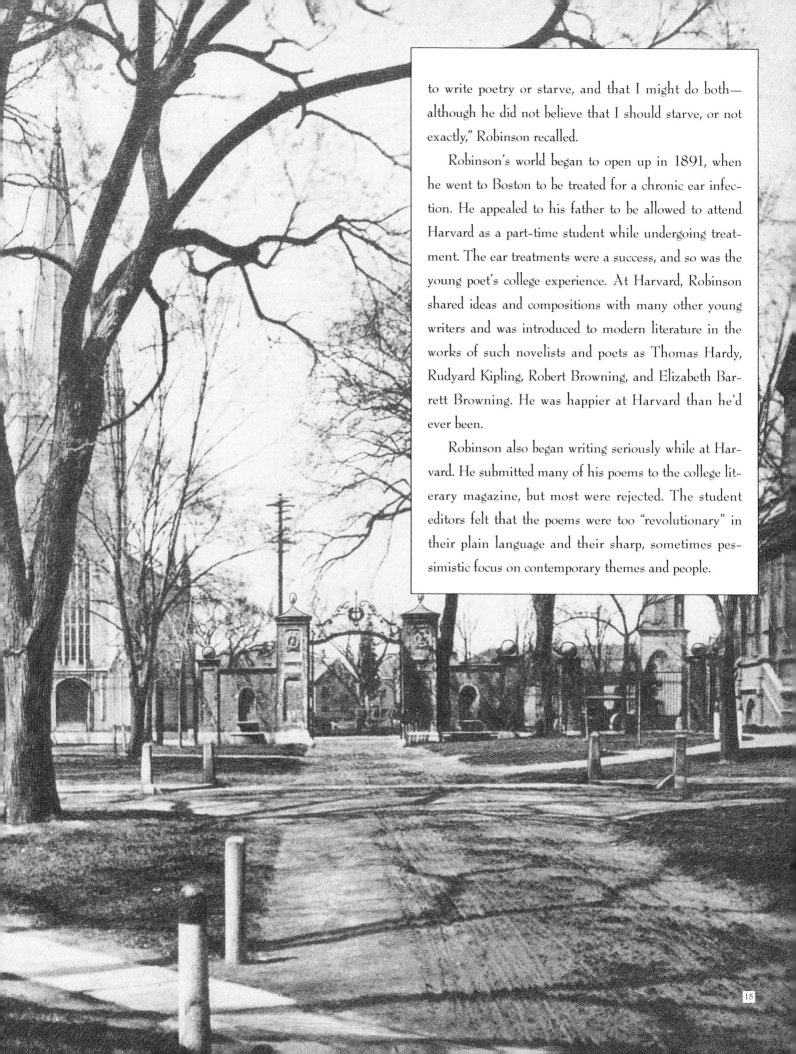

to write poetry or starve, and that I might do both—although he did not believe that I should starve, or not exactly," Robinson recalled.

Robinson's world began to open up in 1891, when he went to Boston to be treated for a chronic ear infection. He appealed to his father to be allowed to attend Harvard as a part-time student while undergoing treatment. The ear treatments were a success, and so was the young poet's college experience. At Harvard, Robinson shared ideas and compositions with many other young writers and was introduced to modern literature in the works of such novelists and poets as Thomas Hardy, Rudyard Kipling, Robert Browning, and Elizabeth Barrett Browning. He was happier at Harvard than he'd ever been.

Robinson also began writing seriously while at Harvard. He submitted many of his poems to the college literary magazine, but most were rejected. The student editors felt that the poems were too "revolutionary" in their plain language and their sharp, sometimes pessimistic focus on contemporary themes and people.

RICHARD CORY

*W*henever Richard Cory went down town,

We people on the pavement looked at him:

He was a gentleman from sole to crown,

Clean favored, and imperially slim.

And he was always quietly arrayed,

And he was always human when he talked;

But still he fluttered pulses when he said,

"Good-morning," and he glittered when he walked.

And he was rich—yes, richer than a king—

And admirably schooled in every grace:

In fine, we thought that he was everything

To make us wish that we were in his place.

So on we worked, and waited for the light,

And went without the meat, and cursed the bread;

And Richard Cory, one calm summer night,

Went home and put a bullet through his head.

From *The Children of the Night*

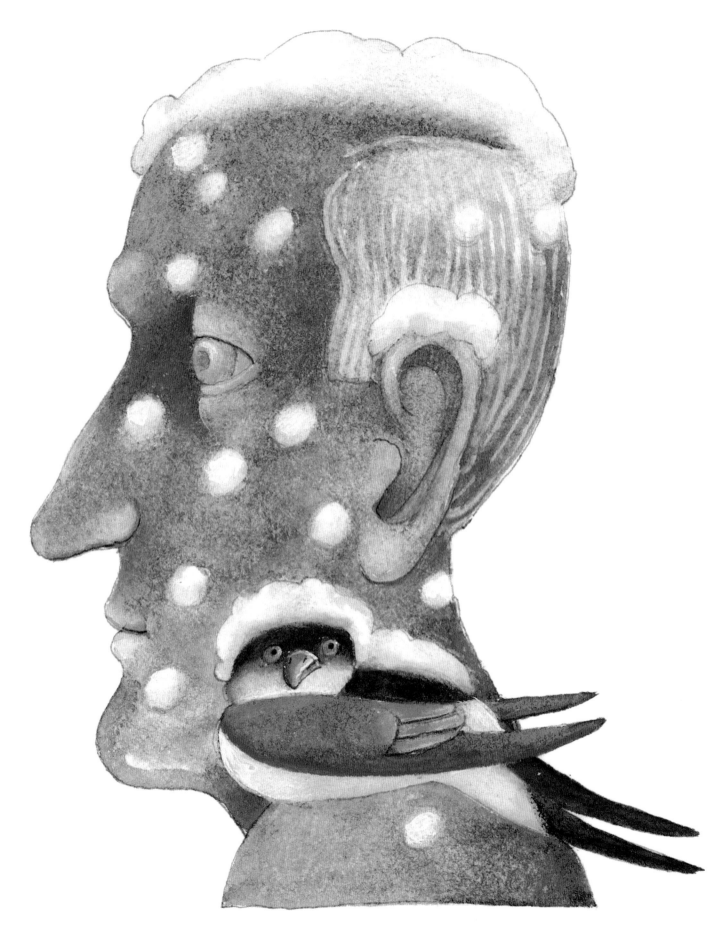

*R*obinson's Harvard education ended abruptly after two years. During that time his father died, and the family lost much of its money in the economic depression of 1893. There were other problems at home as well. His brother Dean had been unable to overcome his drug addiction and was himself slowly dying. His brother Herman, devastated by business failures, was becoming an alcoholic. Ironically, the two "shining lights" of the Robinson clan had flickered considerably, and it would be up to Edwin to achieve whatever success the family might have.

The family held meetings to discuss what Edwin should do with his life. His mother felt he was too much of a dreamer and would never achieve anything. His sister-in-law Emma, Herman's wife, disagreed, announcing that the young man was destined for something special. "God will take care of him," she insisted.

Emma had been Robinson's friend for many years, even before she married Herman. In fact, one of Robinson's biographers, Chard Powers Smith, believes that the poet, who never married, was haunted throughout much of his life by his love for Emma and jealousy of Herman. Several of his poems describe lost or unrequited love or love triangles in which one man longs for another's wife.

Possibly swayed by Emma's confidence in Edwin, the family did not object strenuously when the young man at last announced aloud his plans to be a writer. "Writing has been my dream ever since I was old enough to lay a plan for an air castle," he wrote to a friend in October 1893. "Now for the first time I have something like a favorable opportunity and this winter I shall make a beginning."

Robinson's parents, Edward and Mary.

Let him answer as he will,

Or be lightsome as he may,

Now nor after shall he say

Worn-out words enough to kill,

Or to lull down by their craft,

Doubt, that was born yesterday,

When he lied and when she laughed.

Let him find another name

For the starlight on the snow,

Let him teach her till she know

That all seasons are the same,

And all sheltered ways are fair,—

Still, wherever she may go,

Doubt will have a dwelling there.

From *The Town Down the River*

*F*or the next three years, Robinson sat in his study, reading and writing. Poems emerged from his mind and pen slowly and with painstaking effort. He noted that his verses "ought to go like bees" but "want to go like camels." He told a friend, "It is hunting for hours after one word and not getting it that plays the devil with a man's gray matter."

Robinson focused his poems not on nature or classical subjects, as was common at the time, but on the "tragedies" of ordinary people who might reside in a New England town such as Gardiner. He coined a name for his fictional place—Tilbury Town. Many of his most famous poems focus on the emptiness of the lives of Tilbury Town's residents.

By 1896, Robinson had put together a collection of more than forty poems, which he sent off to several publishers, each of whom rejected it. Feeling that his work still deserved to be read, the poet decided to pub-lish the collection himself. He paid fifty-two dollars to the Riverside Press in Cambridge for a printing of 312 volumes of *The Torrent and the Night Before.*

A few weeks before the book came out, Robinson's mother died suddenly of a very contagious disease known as "black diphtheria." While working through his grief, Robinson sent out copies of his new book to critics around the country. The reviews were mixed, but enough were favorable to encourage Robinson to keep writing. His second collection, *The Children of the Night,* came out in 1897 and was published at the expense of one of the poet's admirers.

Both books dealt with themes of modern life. One theme, possibly reflecting on the business failures of his father and brother, was the shallowness of materialism. Another was the search for affirmation of God's existence in a disquieting world. Still a third subject Robinson explored was the fickleness of love.

Providence, Rhode Island, in the 1880s.

"Where are you going to-night, to-night,—
    Where are you going, John Evereldown?
There's never the sign of a star in sight,
    Nor a lamp that's nearer than Tilbury Town.
Why do you stare as a dead man might?
Where are you pointing away from the light?
And where are you going to-night, to-night,—
    Where are you going, John Evereldown?"

"Right through the forest, where none can see,
    There's where I'm going, to Tilbury Town.
The men are asleep,—or awake, may be,—
    But the women are calling John Evereldown.
Ever and ever they call for me,
And while they call can a man be free?
So right through the forest, where none can see,
    There's where I'm going, to Tilbury Town."

"But why are you going so late, so late,—
    Why are you going, John Evereldown?
Though the road be smooth and the way be straight,
    There are two long leagues to Tilbury Town.
Come in by the fire, old man, and wait!
Why do you chatter out there by the gate?
And why are you going so late, so late,—
    Why are you going, John Evereldown?"

"I follow the women wherever they call,—
    That's why I'm going to Tilbury Town.
God knows if I pray to be done with it all,
    But God is no friend to John Evereldown.
So the clouds may come and the rain may fall,
The shadows may creep and the dead men crawl,—
But I follow the women wherever they call,
    And that's why I'm going to Tilbury Town."

From *The Children of the Night*

*I*n 1902 Robinson moved to New York City, where he remained for most of the rest of his life. He tried to support himself through his writing but found that he also had to work odd jobs to pay for rent and food. One of his jobs was as a timekeeper for workers building New York's first subways. Robinson hated going underground into the dark, gaseous tunnels and began drinking heavily as a way to endure the experience. Unfortunately, his dependence on alcohol lasted long after his subway job ended.

In 1905 Robinson gained an unlikely champion—U.S. President Theodore Roosevelt. Roosevelt's son had come across a copy of *The Children of the Night* in his prep school and recommended it to his father. The president liked the poems so much that he wrote a favorable review of Robinson's work in the literary magazine *The Outlook*. The review had both good and bad results. On the positive side, several magazines and newspapers began to accept Robinson's submissions more readily. On the negative side, some critics objected to the president's acting as a poetry reviewer and as a result directed harsh attacks on Robinson's work.

Roosevelt also helped solve another of Robinson's problems—the need for money. He offered the poet a position in the New York Office of the Collector of Customs. Robinson made brief daily appearances in the office and collected a modest paycheck. Meanwhile, he continued to labor away at both poetry and plays. For the first time in his years in New York, he was not living in near poverty. When Roosevelt failed to win reelection in 1908, however, Robinson once again found himself without a steady income.

Theodore Roosevelt, c. 1902.

Come away! come away! there's a frost along the marshes,
And a frozen wind that skims the shoal where it shakes the dead black water;
There's a moan across the lowland and a wailing through the woodland
Of a dirge that sings to send us back to the arms of those that love us.
There is nothing left but ashes now where the crimson chills of autumn
Put off the summer's languor with a touch that made us glad

For the glory that is gone from us, with a flight we cannot follow,
To the slopes of other valleys and the sounds of other shores.

Come away! come away! you can hear them calling, calling,
Calling us to come to them, and roam no more.
Over there beyond the ridges and the land that lies between us,
There's an old song calling us to come!

(continued)

Come away! come away!—for the scenes we leave

behind us

Are barren for the lights of home and a flame that's

young forever;

And the lonely trees around us creak the warning of

the nightwind,

That love and all the dreams of love are away

beyond the mountains.

The songs that call for us to-night, they have called

for men before us,

And the winds that blow the message, they have blown

ten thousand years;

But this will end our wander-time, for we know the joy

that waits us

In the strangeness of home-coming, and a woman's

waiting eyes.

Come away! come away! there is nothing now to

cheer us –

Nothing now to comfort us, but love's road home: –

Over there beyond the darkness there's a window

gleams to greet us,

And a warm hearth waits for us within.

Come away! come away!—or the roving fiend will

hold us,

And make us all to dwell with him to the end of

human faring:

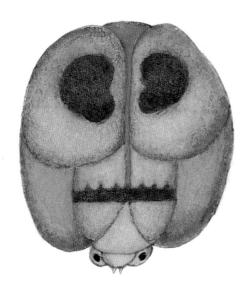

There are no men yet may leave him when his

hands are clutched upon them,

There are none will own his enmity, there are none

will call him brother.

So we'll be up and on the way, and the less we

boast the better

For the freedom that God gave us and the dread we do

not know:—

The frost that skips the willow-leaf will again be back

to blight it,

And the doom we cannot fly from is the doom

we do not see.

Come away! come away! there are dead men all

around us –

Frozen men that mock us with a wild, hard laugh

That shrieks and sinks and whimpers in the shrill

November rushes,

And the long fall wind on the lake.

From The Children of the Night

In 1910 Robinson published a new collection of short poems called *The Town Down the River*. Unlike his earlier work, these poems focused on characters in the big city—New York—rather than the small town. The best remembered of these characters, the scornful, sighing Miniver Cheevy, illustrated many of Robinson's feelings about materialism and false appearance.

The new book was a success with the critics but not with the public. Few copies were sold, and Robinson believed that he might indeed end up starving as a poet, as Dr. Schumann had forewarned.

The following year, ravaged by poor health, fatigue, and heavy drinking, Robinson accepted an invitation to spend a summer at the MacDowell Colony, an artists' retreat in New Hampshire. Living in the peaceful rural surroundings of the MacDowell family's Hillcrest Estate with other writers and musicians rejuvenated the poet and helped him end his dependence on alcohol. He was to spend twenty-four consecutive summers at the Colony, and most of his later work was drafted in New Hampshire and then laboriously completed in New York.

New York City's Hoffman House Bar, popular among businessmen around the turn of the century.

MINIVER CHEEVY

*M*iniver Cheevy, child of scorn,
    Grew lean while he assailed the seasons;
He wept that he was ever born,
    And he had reasons.

Miniver loved the days of old
    When swords were bright and steeds were prancing;
The vision of a warrior bold
    Would set him dancing.

Miniver sighed for what was not,
    And dreamed, and rested from his labors;
He dreamed of Thebes and Camelot,
    And Priam's neighbors.

Miniver mourned the ripe renown
    That made so many a name so fragrant;
He mourned Romance, now on the town,
    And Art, a vagrant.

Miniver loved the Medici,
    Albeit he had never seen one;
He would have sinned incessantly
    Could he have been one.

Miniver cursed the commonplace
    And eyed a khaki suit with loathing;
He missed the mediæval grace
    Of iron clothing.

Miniver scorned the gold he sought,
    But sore annoyed was he without it;
Miniver thought, and thought, and thought,
    And thought about it.

Miniver Cheevy, born too late,
    Scratched his head and kept on thinking;
Miniver coughed, and called it fate,
    And kept on drinking.

From *The Town Down the River*

During his third summer in New Hampshire, Robinson began working on his most important group of poems thus far. The collection had two major inspirations. One was the depression the poet felt at the start of World War I. Robinson believed that the coming of war illustrated the failure of materialism and the need for spiritual answers in the world. His second inspiration occurred while watching a sunset on the peak of Monadnock, a mountain near Hillcrest. He imagined that a man was standing atop the mountain, bathed in the rays of the sun and exposed to the "light of wisdom" that revealed the depressed state of the world. The vision led to a long poem entitled "The Man Against the Sky," which Robinson considered his most complete work yet.

"The Man Against the Sky" became the title poem in Robinson's next volume, which appeared in bookstores in 1916. This new collection earned him wide respect from critics and poets who praised him for the depth of his ideas and the simplicity of his style. Ironically, those were the same qualities that his classmates at Harvard and early reviewers had criticized more than twenty years before.

Robinson hoped that the reception for *The Man Against the Sky* would lead to enough royalties to help him live in relative comfort. He wasn't looking to become rich; in fact, he had once told an interviewer that a poet shouldn't need more than one thousand dollars a year to live. Yet sales of his work did not bring him even that much money. Several of Robinson's friends took the matter of his poverty in hand. They created an anonymous trust fund that would provide him with twelve hundred dollars a year to begin with and fifteen hundred dollars a year by the early 1920s. The gift made it possible for Robinson to concentrate on his writing and not worry about housing and food.

An engraving of Mount Washington, New Hampshire.

THE MAN AGAINST THE SKY

Lines 1–22

*B*etween me and the sunset, like a dome

Against the glory of a world on fire,

Now burned a sudden hill,

Bleak, round, and high, by flame-lit height made higher,

With nothing on it for the flame to kill

Save one who moved and was alone up there

To loom before the chaos and the glare

As if he were the last god going home

Unto his last desire.

Dark, marvelous, and inscrutable he moved on

Till down the fiery distance he was gone,

Like one of those eternal, remote things

That range across a man's imaginings

When a sure music fills him and he knows

What he may say thereafter to few men,—

The touch of ages having wrought

An echo and a glimpse of what he thought

A phantom or a legend until then;

For whether lighted over ways that save,

Or lured from all repose,

If he go on too far to find a grave,

Mostly alone he goes.

From the collection
The Man Against the Sky

The Long Race

As he approached his fiftieth birthday in 1919, Robinson finally achieved critical, if not financial, success. In its December 21, 1919, issue, *The New York Times Book Review* published a feature article entitled "Poets Celebrate E. A. Robinson's Birthday." The comments were glowing. Fellow New England poet Amy Lowell said, "E. A. R. is poetry. I can think of no other living writer who so consistently dedicated his life to his work. He is a poet for poets." Another contemporary writer, Vachel Lindsay, noted that Robinson, in his ability to tell a complete story in a few lines, was "a novelist distilled into a poet."

Robinson's publishers were so impressed with the *Times* tribute that they agreed to publish a complete collection of his work up to that point, more than six hundred pages of poetry. The publication of his *Collected Poems* had two important effects: It brought his work to the attention of the reading public, and it helped end his impoverishment. The book sold nearly five thousand copies in its first year. It also earned Robinson the 1922 Pulitzer Prize for poetry.

E. A. Robinson

1920

HILLCREST

To Mrs. Edward MacDowell

*N*o sound of any storm that shakes

Old island walls with older seas

Comes here where now September makes

An island in a sea of trees.

Between the sunlight and the shade

A man may learn till he forgets

The roaring of a world remade,

And all his ruins and regrets;

And if he still remembers here

Poor fights he may have won or lost,—

If he be ridden with the fear

Of what some other fight may cost,—

(continued)

If, eager to confuse too soon,

What he has known with what may be,

He reads a planet out of tune

For cause of his jarred harmony,—

If here he venture to unroll

His index of adagios,

And he be given to console

Humanity with what he knows,—

He may by contemplation learn

A little more than what he knew,

And even see great oaks return

To acorns out of which they grew.

He may, if he but listen well,

Through twilight and the silence here,

Be told what there are none may tell

To vanity's impatient ear;

And he may never dare again

Say what awaits him, or be sure

What sunlit labyrinth of pain

He may not enter and endure.

From *The Man Against the Sky*

GENEROSITY

Over the next five years, Robinson produced several collections of short works and two long narrative poems, *The Man Who Died Twice* and *Tristram*. The narratives earned Robinson his second and third Pulitzer Prizes. *Tristram* was based on the tale of Tristram and Isolt, an Irish legend included in the stories about King Arthur and the Knights of the Round Table. Robinson's 4,400-line retelling of the tragic romance was also a remarkable popular success. More than 57,000 copies were sold in one year, "which isn't bad for blank verse," Robinson joked to a friend.

Even though he now had enough money to live comfortably, Robinson did not stop working or living frugally. He gave generously to friends who were in need of funds and donated a new diagnostic laboratory to a hospital in Gardiner in memory of his brother Dean, the doctor whose early death had been brought on by drug addiction.

Robinson in Nantucket, Massachusetts.

$\mathscr{N}$ow and again

A louder fanfare of malicious horns

Would sing down from the festival above him,

Smiting his angry face like a wet clout

That some invisible scullion might have swung,

Too shadowy and too agile to be seized

And flung down on those rocks. Now and again

Came over him a cold soul-retching wave

Of recognition past reality,

Recurrent, vile, and always culminating

In a forbidden vision thrice unholy

Of Mark, his uncle, like a man-shaped goat

Appraising with a small salacious eye,

And slowly forcing into his gaunt arms,

And all now in a few impossible hours

That were as possible as pain and death,

The shuddering unreal miracle of Isolt,

Which was as real as torture to the damned

In hell, or in Cornwall. Before long now

That music and that wordless murmuring

Of distant men and women, who divined

As much or little as they might, would cease;

The mocking lights above him would go out;

There would be silence; and the King would hold

Isolt—Isolt of the dark eyes—Isolt

Of the patrician passionate helplessness—

Isolt of the soft waving blue-black hair—

Isolt of Ireland—in his vicious arms

And crush the bloom of her resisting life

On his hot, watery mouth, and overcome

The protest of her suffering silk skin

With his crude senile claws. And it was he,

Tristram, the loud-accredited strong warrior,

Tristram, the loved of women, the harp-player,

Tristram, the learned Nimrod among hunters,

Tristram, the most obedient imbecile

And humble servant of King Mark his uncle,

Who had achieved all this. For lack of sight

And sense of self, and imperturbably,

He had achieved all this and might do more,

No doubt, if given the time. Whereat he cursed

Himself again, and his complacent years

Of easy blindness. Time had saved for him

The flower that he had not the wit to seize

And carry a few leagues across the water,

Till when he did so it was his no more,

And body and soul were sick to think of it.

From *Tristram*

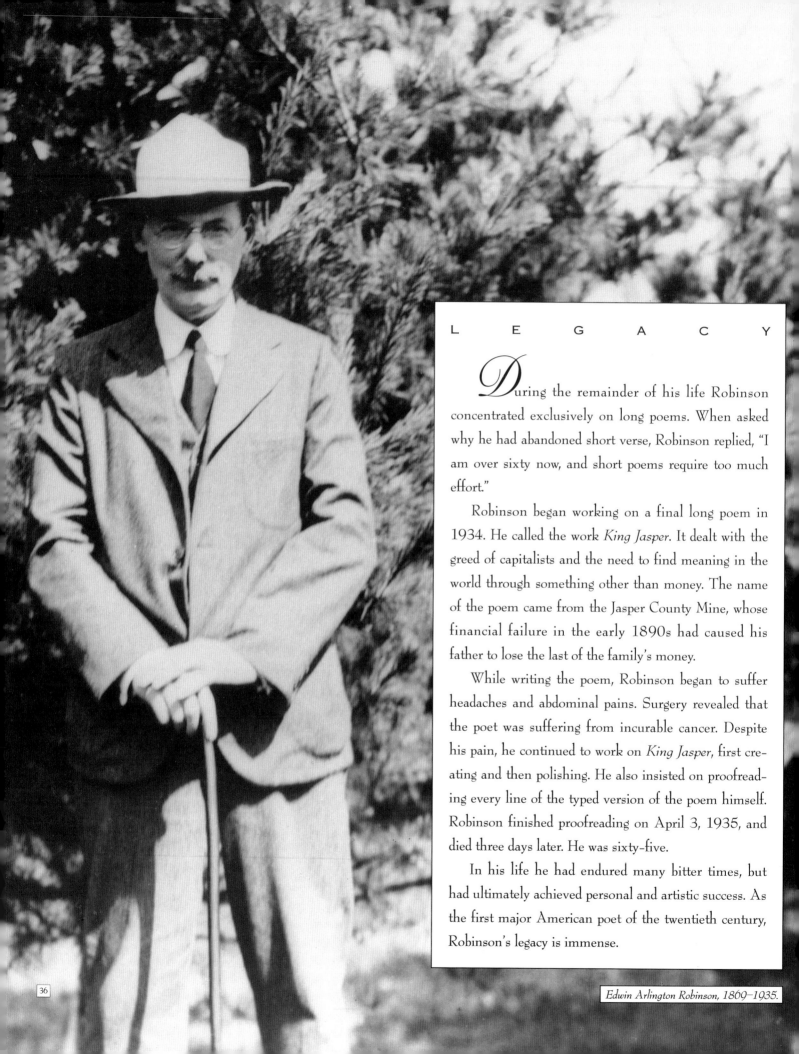

During the remainder of his life Robinson concentrated exclusively on long poems. When asked why he had abandoned short verse, Robinson replied, "I am over sixty now, and short poems require too much effort."

Robinson began working on a final long poem in 1934. He called the work *King Jasper*. It dealt with the greed of capitalists and the need to find meaning in the world through something other than money. The name of the poem came from the Jasper County Mine, whose financial failure in the early 1890s had caused his father to lose the last of the family's money.

While writing the poem, Robinson began to suffer headaches and abdominal pains. Surgery revealed that the poet was suffering from incurable cancer. Despite his pain, he continued to work on *King Jasper*, first creating and then polishing. He also insisted on proofreading every line of the typed version of the poem himself. Robinson finished proofreading on April 3, 1935, and died three days later. He was sixty-five.

In his life he had endured many bitter times, but had ultimately achieved personal and artistic success. As the first major American poet of the twentieth century, Robinson's legacy is immense.

Edwin Arlington Robinson, 1869–1935.

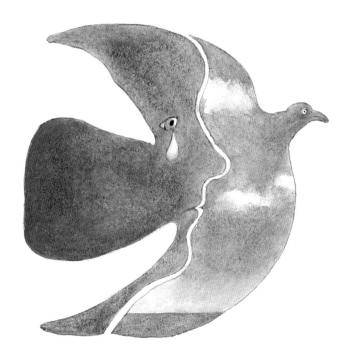

CREDO

I cannot find my way: there is no star

In all the shrouded heavens anywhere;

And there is not a whisper in the air

Of any living voice but one so far

That I can hear it only as a bar

Of lost, imperial music, played when fair

And angel fingers wove, and unaware,

Dead leaves to garlands where no roses are.

No, there is not a glimmer, nor a call,

For one that welcomes, welcomes when he fears,

The black and awful chaos of the night;

For through it all—above, beyond it all—

I know the far-sent message of the years,

I feel the coming glory of the Light.

From *The Children of the Night*

ACKNOWLEDGMENTS

Edited by S. L. Berry and Nancy Loewen
Photo research by Ann Schwab
Design assistant: Mindy Belter

PHOTO CREDITS

The Bettmann Archive
Culver Pictures
Museum of the City of New York, The Byron Collection
North Wind Picture Archives
Special Collections, Colby College Library

POETRY CREDITS

"Dear Friends," "Cliff Klingenhagen," "Ballade of Broken Flutes," "Richard Cory," "John Evereldown," "The Wilderness," and "Credo" from THE CHILDREN OF THE NIGHT by Edwin Arlington Robinson (New York: Charles Scribner's Sons, 1897)

"The Companion" and "Miniver Cheevy" from THE TOWN DOWN THE RIVER by Edwin Arlington Robinson (New York: Charles Scribner's Sons, 1910)

"The Man Against the Sky" and "Hillcrest" from THE MAN AGAINST THE SKY by Edwin Arlington Robinson (New York: Macmillan, 1916)

Excerpt from *Tristram* reprinted with permission of Macmillan Publishing Company from COLLECTED POEMS OF EDWIN ARLINGTON ROBINSON. Copyright 1927 by Edwin Arlington Robinson, renewed 1955 by Ruth Nivison and Barbara R. Holt.

Excerpt from *Roman Bartholow* reprinted with permission of Macmillan Publishing Company from COLLECTED POEMS OF EDWIN ARLINGTON ROBINSON. Copyright 1923 by Edwin Arlington Robinson, renewed 1951 by Ruth Nivison.

SELECTED WORKS BY EDWIN ARLINGTON ROBINSON

POETRY COLLECTIONS
The Children of the Night, 1897
Captain Craig, 1902
The Town Down the River, 1910
The Man Against the Sky, 1916
The Three Taverns, 1920
Avon's Harvest, 1921
Dionysus in Doubt, 1925
Sonnets: 1889–1927, 1928
Nicodemus, 1932

EPIC POEMS
Merlin, 1917
Lancelot, 1920
Roman Bartholow, 1923
The Man Who Died Twice, 1924
Tristram, 1927
The Glory of the Nightingales, 1930
King Jasper, 1935

INDEX

Published by Creative Education
123 South Broad Street, Mankato, Minnesota 56001
Creative Education is an imprint of Creative Education, Inc.
Copyright © 1994 Creative Education, Inc.
International copyrights reserved in all countries.
No part of this book may be reproduced in any form without
written permission from the publisher.
Printed in Italy.
Art Direction: Rita Marshall
Designed by: Stephanie Blumenthal
Illustrations by Etienne Delessert
Library of Congress Cataloging-in-Publication Data
Goodman, Michael E.
    Edwin Arlington Robinson / Michael E. Goodman.
        p.   cm. — (Voices in poetry)
    Includes bibliographical references (p.) and index.
    Summary: Examines the life of the American poet and
presents some of his poems.
    ISBN 0-88682-617-9
    1. Robinson, Edwin Arlington, 1869–1935—Biography—
Juvenile literature. 2. Poets, American—20th century—
Biography—Juvenile literature. 3. Young adult poetry,
American. [1. Robinson, Edwin Arlington, 1869–1935. 2.
Poets, American. 3. American poetry.] I. Title. II. Series:
Voices in poetry (Mankato, Minn.)
PS3535.O25Z665   1993
811'.52—dc20
[B]

93-3374
CIP
AC